CONFLICT

Books by Mukesh Chhajer:

- Random Reflections (2006)
- On Life and Liberation: Essays on Jain Practices and Philosophy (2007)
- Silent Voices (2008, 2012)
- समय के रंग (Samay Ke Rang) (2010, 2012)
- Tirthankar Mahaveer: A Biography in Verse (2010, 2012, 2019)
- Momentary Madness (2012)
- Love's Lies and Other Deceptions (2013)
- आहत आत्माऐं (Aahat Atmaen) (2015)
- मार्ग और मंज़िल (Marg aur Manjil) (2016)
- Quiet Chaos (2017)
- Afternoon Fog (2018)
- Defiance (2018)
- Unlocked (2019)
- Transition (2020)
- A Journey (2021)
- Gaze (2022)
- A Visitor (2023)
- श्रीकृष्ण लीला प्रसंग (Shri Krishna Lila Prasang) (2023)
- Conflict (2024)
- श्री ब्रज लीला (Shri Braj Lila) (2024)

CONFLICT

a collection of poems

by

Mukesh Chhajer

Title: Conflict
Author: Mukesh Chhajer
Language: English

Published: July 07, 2024

Publisher: Mangal Publications

Cover Photograph: Mukesh Chhajer

Copyright © 2024 Mukesh Chhajer
All rights reserved. No part of this book can be reproduced in any form without the prior written permission of the author, except brief excerpts for reviews.

ISBN 13: 978-1-962178-03-7

Conflict -- Mukesh Chhajer

what is today's trend-setter is tomorrow's routine
the newness lasts, but for a few seconds
celebration though runs, many-many months
to fill the gap of, unproductive existence

we engage in the game of, chicken-and-egg
claiming originality where little can be seen
with a constant drumbeat of, innovation and creation
we recycle ideas, at an alarming rate

what we claim lost
        merely a thought misplaced
what we claim gained
        just a momentary acquaintance
with the mindset of an accountant
        we are ever engaged in the bottom line
without realizing, a dollar lost or gained
        does not have the same value, all the time

Conflict -- Mukesh Chhajer

drops which separate from the river
get no respect

drops that originate from the clouds
provide temporary relief

drops which emerge from the void
unleash a flood of bliss

ઝ ♦ ଓ

if tomorrow could be killed
if yesterday could be erased
if today could be stretched
beyond the limits of the mind

all conflicts will become, non-existent

ઝ ♦ ଓ

Conflict -- Mukesh Chhajer

every pain has something to teach
ever pleasure has something to lose
an accountant is only happy
when there are new entries
to add to a balance sheet

ॐ

blame not tomorrow for
        today's sorrow
joy does not overflow
        from yesterday's actions
every moment is a moment
        worth its own satisfaction

ॐ

Conflict -- Mukesh Chhajer

what would a death be if
        life was not feisty
what would a life be if
        death was not waiting
what would a truth be if
        lies were not around
what would a lie be if
        truth did not pose a threat

        ❧ ♦ ☙

a wave is a conflict, of water
        short-lived
a mountain is a conflict, of land
        simmering over a long time
a tornado is a conflict, of air
        momentary
a man is a conflict, of emotions
        over many-many lives

        ❧ ♦ ☙

Conflict -- Mukesh Chhajer

if your days and nights are controlled by
the rising and the setting of the sun without

your education has not yet, begun

                                                        ಇ♦ೢ

if your day begins, with a firm belief
            that I am always right
welcome the opportunities
            that prove it otherwise

if your day begins, with a hesitating thought
            that I cannot get anything right
witness the events as they unfold
            to prove it otherwise

a new day only dawns to highlight
            your weaknesses and shortcomings
there will be no more new days
            once you are perfect

Conflict -- Mukesh Chhajer

it may not happen today or tomorrow
it may even take many-many years or births
at some point when time is tired, it will be forced to reveal
the truth of my existence

in cycles innumerable until then
I must peregrinate
A curse and a blessing, I have
bestowed upon myself

ॐ♦ॐ

what have you earned in a lifespan
        of 40, 60, or 70 years
money, fame, and power; if you respond
        would be a pathetic answer

look deeper, have you earned
        decency, humility, or innocence
if not, I am afraid, you have
        entrapped yourself further into

the sinister play of time

ॐ♦ॐ

Conflict -- Mukesh Chhajer

I broke through many barriers, none though were
               of ego, jealousy, or selfishness
I have erected many walls, none though were
               of humility, compassion, or innocence
I circumvented many mountains, none though were
               of arrogance, greed, or dishonesty
I built many forts, none though were
               of charity, integrity, or dignity

what outcomes will these efforts engender?

               ❧◆☙

a voice rose, from the depth
               of the heart, faint and weak
quickly drowned out by a thud
               of a falling dollar bill

the process is repeated
               every few minutes or days
                             weeks, months, or years
depending upon how closely you are
               paying attention

the gap between its successive
               appearance is proportional inversely
to your own honesty
               integrity and humanity

               ❧◆☙

Conflict -- Mukesh Chhajer

a loud bang, followed by a long silence
        or a constant whisper
to reform a system, one cannot afford
        to merely choose just one extreme

to dig a tunnel, to build a bridge
        big explosions must be followed
                by small skirmishes

☙ ♦ ❧

in front of my bedroom window
        stands a tree, to block
the volleys of the sun
        every morning

day-after-day, week-after-week
        from late spring until early autumn
to protect me from
        being bullied, before losing
                to nature's harsh reality

I though have never even once
        thanked it for its sacrifice

☙ ♦ ❧

Conflict -- Mukesh Chhajer

if bright is the smile but darkness within
if gentle is the touch but harshness within
if sweet is the tongue but bitterness within
will they produce, any outcome beneficial?

I have taken a vow, to be victorious
               in every venture, I engage in
without realizing, the purpose of life is
               to surrender with grace

Conflict -- Mukesh Chhajer

if I had the strength to defeat
anyone in the world in wrestling
who would I wrestle with

if I had the knowledge to defeat
anyone in the world in debate
who would I debate with

if I had the speed to defeat
anyone in the world in sprint
who would I sprint against

at the moment though, I am
falling behind to keep up
with my own self

Conflict -- Mukesh Chhajer

some days, truth is put
            on a pedestal
some days, truth has to suffer
            a humiliating treatment

neither options truth is
            comfortable with
truth merely wishes to be
            allowed to stand on its own

                  ఇ♦ఊ

to honor a pledge is honorable
unless, the pledge itself is dishonorable

to respect an action is respectable
unless, the action itself is disrespectful

to embrace a cause is admirable
unless, the cause itself is despicable

to support a truth is moral
unless, the truth itself is immoral

                  ఇ♦ఊ

Conflict -- Mukesh Chhajer

a piece of bread has limited strength
to a hungry though, it is heaven sent

a glass of water gets hardly noticed
unless you have walked, a mile in the sun

a leafless tree gets no respect
unless it stands, in the middle of a desert

a painful truth gets repeatedly ignored
unless it becomes, a conduit to freedom

ಙ♦ಚ

when yesterdays were today, we said
        we don't care
when todays were tomorrow, we demanded
        their presence right away
with our concerns, disproportionately focused
        on time not present
we bury ourselves deeper in to
        time's cunning trap

ಙ♦ಚ

Conflict -- Mukesh Chhajer

before you step through the gate
to claim the victory
take a moment to reflect
Once claimed, victory will extract
its revenge

in ways and by means you will
never be able to anticipate
Friends will become foes, foes friends
Honors will be bestowed, for reasons unknown

truth will become, a dish flavored
with ever new ingredients
to make it palatable for
reasons selfish

darkness will become, a constant companion
with spotlight shinning, always on you
A tiny lamp with limited oil, can it
light the entire sky

before you step through the gate
to claim the victory
take a moment to reflect

Conflict -- Mukesh Chhajer

words may not say, they are in a hurry
eyes may not express, they are wary
touch is unable, to make a connection when
hearts have separated, even by an inch

in the world today, time is money
tomorrow's deeds today it demands to complete
with tools missing and parts improper
world insists on building a skyscraper, without a foundation

☙◆❧

"If you can adhere to the truth
every moment of every day
you will be saved.", an advice
offered by those who are unwilling

to look within their own selves
They insist, truth is what
they claim to be, anyone
who disagrees or anything

to the contrary, deserves
to rot in hell
for eternity

messiahs of the modern world
wear a thick coat of self-delusion

☙◆❧

Conflict -- Mukesh Chhajer

today did not dawn as it was planned
a train-full of treasures did not
stop in front of my doors

like a surreptitious thief, it
entered my home to rob
me of my precious little
peace and quiet

the story though is not new
or few and far between
every day it repeats to make me wonder
am I being taken for a fool

❈

falling eyesight does not mean
       you are getting old
bulging biceps do not mean
       youth is making a comeback

decline and growth, both serve
       to please their master Time
find a way to distance from either
       to find your own, kingdom

❈

Conflict -- Mukesh Chhajer

in the darkness, hides light
every candle knows, this truth
standing in front of the sun
man though thinks, it is the source

Those who wish to understand
the nature of light, must
ignite a flame within
How can a moon claim
it has found the answer

Conflict -- Mukesh Chhajer

what is unethical, a truth
    suppressed or a lie spread
what is better, a help
    rendered or never asked
what is moral, sacrificing
    others or situation avoided
questions one must consider carefully
    before claiming values

ఌ♦ఎ

what will you lose if you
    gained a bit of arrogance
what will you gain if you
    lost a bit of humility
what will you lose if you
    gained a bit of wealth
what will you gain if you
    lost a bit of compassion

losses and gains are immaterial
    if you remain, a mere witness
a source of great perils, otherwise

ఌ♦ఎ

Conflict -- Mukesh Chhajer

what words have not caused harm even
        how-so-ever sweetly they were spoken
what words have not led to inspiration even
        though the intent was to insult
what words have not been abused even
        though they may be most beautiful

words are at the mercy of
        their messengers

☙◆❧

power is a blessing if you are
        adapt at harnessing
a curse if it corrupts
        your very being

few have shown the strength
        and the courage needed to
                channel power in the right direction
most just get overrun

☙◆❧

Conflict -- Mukesh Chhajer

when values are claimed like
an appliance on a sale
during Christmas or Independence Day
blockbuster blowout with
no interest for next two years

a self-induced coma sets in
which if not fought with
an aggressive dose of realism
quickly spreads to render one
incapable of opening one's eyes

many have already fallen in the trap
many more do every day
an easy fix in the world where
truth is regularly paraded, like a thief

mountains seen on the surface
      of the earth are show-offs
real ones bury themselves deep
      to avoid becoming a roadblock

Conflict -- Mukesh Chhajer

to hunger for fame, one is still anonymous
to hunger for strength, one is till weak
to hunger for wealth, one is still poor
to hunger for power, one is still helpless

hunger is insatiable

०३♦८०

truth was not called to testify
    heaving a sigh of relief
often denigrated, rarely supported
    it would rather remain quiet

until the time when it can
    stand before an impartial jury
Man though cannot be expected to rise
    to such a level

०३♦८०

Conflict -- Mukesh Chhajer

will you die if in return
you are promised, a long-long
life

will you live if in return
you are promised, a miniscule
of your own property

we haven't learnt to live
or die, thus the question
has assumed importance

for those who have, birth
and death are merely random stops
along a journey, long

ଓ♦ଡ

vitality is not vital when
               you have nothing to offer
strength and power are useful
               only when goals are virtuous

too often in the world today though
               power itself has become the end
with the strength of deception, one must
               grab it at any cost

ଓ♦ଡ

Conflict -- Mukesh Chhajer

a flag unfurled may have
                a long arduous tale
or merely a boastful reminder
                that I am privileged

with little to distinguish once
                the flag is unfurled
we often misjudge the real purpose
                behind the act of defiance

                        ॐ♦ॐ

share the sorrow, share the joy
share every pleasure, the world has to offer
share though not, the secrets of the silence
once disclosed, their value will be lost

                        ॐ♦ॐ

Conflict -- Mukesh Chhajer

unanchored thoughts, look for easy targets
unanchored minds, for broken man
unanchored values, don't even care
who are being crushed, under their weight

ଓ ♦ ଅ

to wealth I did not ask
        why have you come
for poverty though, my
        doors were closed

to fame I did not ask
        why have you come
for anonymity though, my
        doors were closed

to power I did not ask
        why have you come
for helplessness though, my
        doors were closed

wealth, fame, and power; having
        used me for their purpose
left even without a note while
        poverty, anonymity, and helplessness
            still stand at the door

ଓ ♦ ଅ

Conflict -- Mukesh Chhajer

last of the last, even the sun
is afraid to touch
when man with wealth and power
become blinded by arrogance

༄ ♦ ༄

the earth would not survive
even a day if
the sun and the moon decide
to go their separate ways

the sun would not survive
even a day if
its elders did not give it space
to frolic and grow

the Milky-way would not survive
even a day if
all its siblings had decided to
stay together

the universe would not survive
even a day if
I had not decided to
open my eyes

༄ ♦ ༄

Conflict -- Mukesh Chhajer

all declarations are a façade
all proclamations are a farce
all assertions are merely an attempt
to cover one's nakedness

the true-self never has any need
to proclaim, declare, or assert
a veil is needed only if
one feels ashamed

in a distant past, the earth
was merely a blob, of hot
lava and noxious gases

over time, with patience and diligence
it managed to become
a beautiful flower

a journey long and arduous with
many setbacks and heartache
along the way

once again, the earth is facing
a similar crisis, only this time
the culprits are, its own children

Conflict -- Mukesh Chhajer

to a drop, its world is limited
until it becomes a part
of a river

to a river, its world is limited
until it becomes a part
of an ocean

to an ocean, its world is limited
until it becomes a part
of the earth

to the earth, its world is limited
until it becomes a part
of the universe

only by surrendering does one achieve
greatness

༄ ♦ ༄

I don't speak yet, words
      have become a constant companion
I don't act yet, actions
      have become my signature
I don't think yet, thoughts
      control my presence

a parasitic existence

༄ ♦ ༄

Conflict -- Mukesh Chhajer

when God said, "Be"
        I became
now God wonders, how will it
        undo the damage

        ಌ ♦ ಌ

a narrow stream, a rarely
        traveled trail
a barely sprouting bud, a sapling
        fragile

at every step, their existence
        is at stake
at every step, they are filled with
        a potential infinite

        ಌ ♦ ಌ

Conflict -- Mukesh Chhajer

a rose is neither red nor white
a rose is merely an impression
created by one's eyes with the help
of a clever mind

to attach it a value, based upon
what it appears
makes it easy for the mind to
lead one astray

to lose to a truth may be painful
                but honorable
to lose to a lie may be beneficial
                but deplorable

to lose either would be
                inconsequential if
you have risen above
                your limited self

Conflict -- Mukesh Chhajer

to lose is the destiny
to win, a minor setback
those who have lost completely
never complain of being, powerless

death does not defy life
nor life death
as long as one shows
respect, to both

man though has diverted from
this simple truth
forcing life and death to
engage in a treacherous battle

Conflict -- Mukesh Chhajer

all truths have to compromise
when it comes to mankind
Man though is delusional enough
to claim, it has the power
to embrace the absolute truth
while paying least attention
to the ensuing disasters

a circus in the evening, performed
for a few days every year
is a welcome relief

forced to watch it though
every moment of every day
is nerve-wracking

Conflict -- Mukesh Chhajer

to the brink and back, if repeated
often, will eventually result in
an irreversible step

with confidence running amuck
and intelligence crushed under arrogance
a day is not far enough when

the nation and the world will find itself
staring in the face of an unmitigated disaster
Don't you dare though to wake up

the leaders, too busy they are
admiring themselves, in a mirror

(Solar eclipse August 2017)

darkness will descent, to celebrate
a celestial event, in broad daylight

the sun, a proud and fearless leader
will surrender, albeit, only for a few
brief moments, to one of its knights

for the entertainment of its subjects
Scores have lined up along the way
many-many more will view this
through a marvel called Internet

the view, full or partial
will be remembered for its
spectacular display

Conflict -- Mukesh Chhajer

God, being dragged in the affairs of man
must wonder at the wisdom of
its own creation

love, compassion, truthfulness; God
dispersed in abundance, to be
used with care and intelligence
have turned along the way in to

selfishness, greed, hunger for power
and over-the-top self-righteousness
A silent self-reflection has been overthrown by
demands to force others, to follow our way

it is not in the hands of God anymore
man thinks itself self-sufficient
to judge and punish those who disagree
with God's command, as man thinks they should be

if today's victory becomes
tomorrow's truth
man is running on
a slippery slope

Conflict -- Mukesh Chhajer

are you a man of values if you
pay visit to a house of worship, regularly

are you a woman of values if you
donate to a charity, regularly

are you a person of values if you
lend a helping hand to a needy, regularly

if all the while you are constantly wondering
how will it benefit me, personally

ଔ♦ଃ

silence won't descend until you have
        learnt, what noise is
beauty won't be understood until you have
        experienced, ugliness in abundance
victories won't accumulate until you have
        tasted, defeats repeatedly
truth won't dawn until you have
        dissected, lies to their barebones

ଔ♦ଃ

Conflict -- Mukesh Chhajer

what is worse, a truth or a lie
think for a moment, before you opine

for a child, moon is in a bucket
            filled with water
to a lover, the universe resides
            in the eyes of the beloved

what is worse, a truth or a lie
think for a moment, before you opine

☙ ◆ ❧

as to the heaven, there are
            many roads
none though goes through
            streets named Dishonesty, Selfishness
                or Greed

☙ ◆ ❧

Conflict -- Mukesh Chhajer

panic is a sign, of unripeness
hoarding, that of lack of faith
sharing is a sign, of growth
witnessness, of having overcome
all barriers

ஐ♦ஓ

despite all our efforts, truth
        has managed to survive
in spite of all our efforts, lies
        have short lives
man though with increasingly
        selfish and myopic views
continues to strip humanity
        of every vestige of dignity

ஐ♦ஓ

Conflict -- Mukesh Chhajer

another monster hurricane
to turn a major city in to
a miles wide swimming pool

man though is deaf and blind
redoubling its efforts to continue to move
in the direction that can only lead to
greater and bigger disasters

obsessed with being right, at every
step of the way
man has forgotten that to take a step back
sometimes is essential to make progress
in the right direction

ಜ ♦ ೞ

world has only one purpose
to rob man, of its arrogance
a task, alas, it finds
too onerous

ಜ ♦ ೞ

Conflict -- Mukesh Chhajer

world has only one purpose
to rob man, of its innocence
a task, alas, it finds
too easy, to accomplish

truth is vibrant and alive but
only when it is able to move
freely, under the open skies

truth has no shelf-life

Conflict -- Mukesh Chhajer

man's biggest challenge is not
poverty of wealth or of mind
it is the over-abundance of
ethical and moral self-righteousness
that threatens to send it to
its gallows

"Thank you, Lord", what
an obnoxious phrase
Has man already risen
to His level

it would be considered polite
and courteous to thank those
who differ from you only
in degrees

does man think it belongs
in the same category?

Conflict -- Mukesh Chhajer

from whom we receive all
        a thank you is too rude
from whom we receive all
        a sorry is too crude
from whom we receive all
        just be without deception
not that we have the power to
        create a veil, thick enough

ಚ ♦ ಬ

if satisfied you are not, ask
what is the source of
this restlessness

if happy you are not, ask
what is the source of
this unpleasantness

if content you are not, ask
what is the source of
this greed

if honest you are not, ask
what is the source of
this misdeed

if you are courageous enough
you will find that at the root
lies selfishness

ಚ ♦ ಬ

Conflict -- Mukesh Chhajer

in good times, everyone
appears a genius
chaff gets separated from the grains
in the times of crises

whether on a journey through a rough sea
whether on a track through a steep hill
whether on a quest for the personal best
dishonesty, greed, and selfishness will never
hesitate to show off, their ugly faces

all my thoughts are personal
thoughts themselves though have
no such reservations

in bed, with anyone who is willing
to entertain, they spawn a generation
most promiscuous

Conflict -- Mukesh Chhajer

if you lose a tooth, eating
for a few weeks may become
a conscious effort

those who lose an arm or a leg
have to live with the consequences
a little longer

those who lose morality and ethics though
never seem to slow down
even for a second

What has left was due to leave
what arrived was also destined
instead of trying to control the traffic
why don't you just, step aside

Conflict -- Mukesh Chhajer

from behind the mask, signals umpire
Strike
Batter cringes, pitcher heaves
short-stop and outfielders give
a tepid clap

the ball makes a round from
the catcher, to the first base
then to the second and back
to the pitcher for him

to restart his routine
Arms raised, knee chest high
pirouetting to send cameras
and fans in to, a high pitched shrill

a game of summer, with its
languid pace, once considered
an ideal pastime when the sun
overstays every day

has now-a-days become known
more for the contract disputes
and steroid use instead of
a spectacular catch

ಣ♦ಐ

Conflict -- Mukesh Chhajer

when a thought reveals itself
be careful, before embracing it
a thought never makes itself available
without a selfish motive

ಚ♦ಐ

a yesterday is just today
               gone awry
a tomorrow is just today
               still innocent
today is just a teenager
               still searching for a meaning
                           in life
without proper guidance, it will
               make choices, unwise

ಚ♦ಐ

Conflict -- Mukesh Chhajer

in the name of progress, let us not
        sacrifice decency
in the name of progress, let us not
        sacrifice honesty
in the name of progress, let us not
        sacrifice humility
without them, otherwise, nothing
        would be left of humanity

ෆ♦ෂ

if ego were to be a twig
one could easily break it
a mighty trunk though requires
special equipment

if ego were to be a tiny hill
one could easily conquer it
to scale the Mount Everest requires
special training

if ego were to be a narrow stream
one could easily walk through it
to cross an ocean requires
a mighty ship

if ego were to be a blooming garden
one could easily stroll there for an hour
to cross a minefield requires
an armored vehicle

ෆ♦ෂ

Conflict -- Mukesh Chhajer

a stone has patience
a tree, forbearance
a river is without
ego or arrogance

mountains rise
oceans have depth
land has the capacity
to support a great burden

every element of the nature
has a lesson to teach
only if man has the capacity
to look beyond itself

Conflict -- Mukesh Chhajer

a small boat at the sea
capsized by waves unseen
in the middle of an ocean
full of traffic

its shouts were unheard
its sight was unseen
its immersion was unheralded
as a casualty of the storm

now it resides, neither
on the surface nor at the bottom
untethered and without a paddle
it has been given the freedom

to disappear into the oblivion
of its own creation

Conflict -- Mukesh Chhajer

fate did not offer
fate did not rob
fate merely said, I bring
what was in store

good-or-bad, pleasant-or-painful
fate walked on the stage, as cued
to merely reveal what has been
buried, without proper resolution

ಙ♦ಜ

in the hands of man, time
      itself has become a slave
controlled by watches and clocks
      not a moment is free, to go by
          unnoticed

man, with its incessant need
      to control rivers, trees
          air, fire, and land, thinks
time is just one of these
      inanimate objects which it can control
          with the help of its own cunningness

a self-delusion, costly and dangerous

ಙ♦ಜ

Conflict -- Mukesh Chhajer

layers upon layers of cosmetic products
cannot change what is in one's heart
world though claims, all one needs
is a make-up artist, to make one divine

calculated, but careless
intelligent, but clueless
strong, yet useless
a world full of morality, selfish

Conflict -- Mukesh Chhajer

when you say, death is a friend
be certain, from death
you will receive, no favoritism

when you say, death is an enemy
be certain, death does not engage
in extracting revenge

death merely arrives at the door
at its predestined time
friend or foe, death has no
                preconceived notion

perform it will, its duties
without any joy or remorse

let lessons learn a lesson when
lessons claim, they are a friend

how often have lessons delivered
their message, without first
knocking one down, a few times

Conflict -- Mukesh Chhajer

and so begins the great debate
with knives and guns, hidden under coat
to neutralize anyone who dares
to challenge

The country will greatly benefit from
what we have proposed
a few million will lose healthcare
a few million bankrupt

but we would have delivered
on the promise we made
out of jealousy, spite
and hatred

benefits will accrue, to those
already privileged by the system
healthcare will be delivered, to those
already healthy and without need

and the rest, good luck finding
a charitable entity who will be
able to provide you with
a few pills

Conflict -- Mukesh Chhajer

it is a myth that death only comes
to take away those who have
exhausted their allotted time
on the earth

now-a-days, even death is engaged in
dishonest business
accidents, shootings, insurgencies and wars
death has invented numerous games

to engage man to do, its bidding
by enticing it in the name of
a fabulous afterlife with
no strings attached

and man, looking for a shortcut to success
eagerly embraces them, without much thought
intelligence, offered to it by God, often
gets abused by turning to, the dark side

☙♦❧

Conflict -- Mukesh Chhajer

intelligence has become an orphan
hope, a beggar
wisdom is being suffocated by
the self-righteousness of man
what use blaming, God for calamities
when man has become expert
in digging its own grave

like an ancient samurai, with
sword in its hand
man is eager, to destroy future
in one single stroke

with commonsense crucified
and honesty banished
life has been reduced to
a game of checkers

Conflict -- Mukesh Chhajer

heaven is under pressure
hell, under duress
man has upended, all
measures for division

it demands freedom, by being arrogant
it demands success, by being obnoxious
it demands love, by being overpowering
it demands fame, by being notorious

all means nature uses to distinguish
between good and evil
find themselves badly mutilated
and mangled

how can heaven and hell then
function without partisan favors

Conflict -- Mukesh Chhajer

we are too eager to celebrate
a day of victory
why not a day of defeat

nothing teaches a lesson better
than when one is forced to lick
a bit of dust

in a strange way, we are the truth
we continue to reject
to complain then of being cheated
by a system we helped invent

like a dam, drinking all the water
or a bank, absconding with the money
we continue to create structure whose
sole purpose is to crash
on our own head

Conflict -- Mukesh Chhajer

what wonders world may endure when
a madman sits on the throne
what we have seen is just a trailer
this movie has, an unpleasant end

waves upon waves of disasters
some natural but most self-inflicted
to create a sense of excitement and suspense
a movie turning in to, a real life

the actors are eager to go even further
to make it the worst you have ever faced
blind, deaf, and dumb, they harken to a time
when man used to live, in caves

except in this version, they will still possess
all their modern comforts

ॐ♦ॐ

Conflict -- Mukesh Chhajer

as God recedes from the streets
and from the hearts of men and women
shouts and megaphones rush
to fill the vacuum

world, accustomed as it is
abhors silence
pushing thus noise deeper and deeper
in to one's consciousness until

man becomes an empty shell
filled with echo
of its own arrogance
A state it finds, most comfortable

ೞ♦ೞ

courage, defined as an ability
to stand up against injustice
is not
long-lasting

today though the meaning has changed
once displayed, you can put it on
as a badge to remind the world
of who you were, while continuing

to engage in behavior
cowardly

ೞ♦ೞ

Conflict -- Mukesh Chhajer

religion today has become
a one-way street
God only cares about the cherry
at the top of a garbage heap

a cut of 5% or 10 or 20
how can God be not pleased
how does it matter to God, how
I managed to collect the treasure

in the bank, savings earn
less than a percent
on the Wall Street, it may
go up to 5 or 7
God is sharing my treasure
without any collateral
how dare God say, you are not
a good citizen

Conflict -- Mukesh Chhajer

at last, the pall-bearers are here
let the journey begin

if life was spent, preparing
for this day
even without a crowd, the parade
will be majestic
With the sun, the moon
and the stars in attendance
nature will present a sight
world will never forget

a miserable event it will
otherwise be
with only shadows and darkness
providing company
A dull glitter of a fake gold
can barely withstand the heat
how will then bogus victories
produce a joyous parade

dust does not settle
       on a flowing stream
even a pyramid otherwise
       is no match

Conflict -- Mukesh Chhajer

even in a desert, you may find
                a lonely bush
even in a garden, you may find
                a dry patch
even during the day, you may find
                a spot of darkness
even during the midnight, you may find
                a ray of light

in a normal life, exceptions are
                just that, exceptions
they become the norm though
                in a life exceptional

                        ☙ ◆ ❧

as real as I may be, there is
a part of me even I find
hard to believe

a person, a male, an instructor
                easy they are, in the eyes of the world
a thinker, a writer, sincere
                some may even grant me that
spiritual, valuable, essential
                now I am hanging by a thread
but to say that I am divine
                stretches even my imagination

                        ☙ ◆ ❧

Conflict -- Mukesh Chhajer

goals are never good unless
you have whetted them
for motives

advice is never good unless
you have cleansed yourself
of selfishness

actions are never good unless
you have acted devoid
of greed

Conflict -- Mukesh Chhajer

(Las Vegas shooting 2017)

a man, a retired man
a retired white man
the announcement breathed
a sigh of relief

and the tone changed abruptly
terrorist, criminal, or a beast
to a lone wolf with deep-seated grudges

the planning had been immaculate
with cameras to warn of incoming danger
and a cache of arms, surreptitiously smuggled
to the suspect's hotel room

then on a cool breezy day
the mayhem began
perched above in his hotel room
spraying bullets on concert goers

dead, wounded, and traumatized
as if a rerun of something
that has occurred all too often
with equally predictable, responses

the only difference this time
he is a white man

Conflict -- Mukesh Chhajer

if I can catch tomorrow in the act
        banishing it would be, a child's play
aware of my intensions, even before
        I become cognizant
tomorrow lulls me into, a false sense
        of being in control

ങ♦ഌ

dare not change the narrative
of a recent mass shooting
dead must be buried, wounded
must be healed, before

we can have any, meaningful conversation
A repeat of the argument, we have
heard often enough, to make one
even skip the whole episode

society is on a rerun binge
we though do not have the power, to resurrect
with every repeat, a new cast must participate
and fresh graves become, the only lasting outcome

ങ♦ഌ

Conflict -- Mukesh Chhajer

a silence is a silence only if
                mind cooperates
turning off television, running away
                to a far-off cave, or locking
all doors and windows of your house is
                merely a pretense

ಚ♦ಜ

a lion, a cheetah, a rabbit, or a dog
none have the power, to change their fate
with the power to change, the fate of the planet
man bickers about minor discomforts

lions don't deceive lions, rabbits don't stab rabbits
even dogs, cats, and ants live by the rules
stuffed with complex superiority, man goes out of its way
to insult and abuse, its own kind

ಚ♦ಜ

Conflict -- Mukesh Chhajer

a foothold is never lost or gained
a foothold is merely an illusion
for those who have lost connection
with their own self

if you are one, with The One
and your only one
even the vast empty universe becomes
a solid and sturdy support

a strong castle, a tall building
a cave dug under a high mountain
otherwise is merely a house
of cards

Conflict -- Mukesh Chhajer

growth now has potential
only in Silicon
Carbon has surrendered
its reign

Carbon and Nitrogen, surrounded
by Hydrogen at-will
have clogged human brain

greed, selfishness, jealousy, hatred
the nefarious cousins of Carbon and its brethren
have turned human blood into
a poison

Silicon though is still innocent
like a child, it does not yet understand
"fire" and fire are not the same
It still needs Carbon, to help it
navigate through the maze

Conflict -- Mukesh Chhajer

when I claimed, death
is merely a stop along
the destination
death was not amused

to be thus humiliated
it now must seek
revenge, it has befriended
breath

with every exhalation now
it threatens to embrace
with every inhalation, it reminds
I am right behind

the only escape, let breath
become suspend
without its companion, death
will be forced to leave me
alone

Conflict -- Mukesh Chhajer

dark is not the night
nor the day bright
their occurrence the sun
does not define

when the heart is simple
and motives pure
a light will burn bright
even on a dark night

at last, I have become
a thought-desert
Rarely does one come
Once here though it gets lost

in the shifting sand dunes
going round-and round until
exhaustion takes over

and it slowly becomes
its own tomb
like the Great Sphinx

will it ever be rediscovered
or remain buried forever
Once caught in my orb

it loses its freedom

Conflict -- Mukesh Chhajer

I said, "Let there be light"
expecting a dramatic shift
the universe went about
its way, though a bit amused

imagine if it had to respond
to every whim-and-fancy
of an insignificant being

ॐ ♦ ॐ

don't lose the truth, teeth though
are matters, altogether different
we though are busy polishing teeth
while truth gets soiled, every minute

ॐ ♦ ॐ

Conflict -- Mukesh Chhajer

I did not lose, nor won
world though wasn't satisfied
with the outcome

I did not gain, nor lose
world though complained
it's unfair

I did not claim, nor disowned
world though could not tolerate
such innocence

I did not feel elated, nor dejected
world though felt
threatened

I did not accept, nor gave
world called me an ingrate
buffoon

Conflict -- Mukesh Chhajer

where would tomorrow be, were it
    not for today to be, generous and kind
where would lies be, were it
    not for the truth to be, gentle and vibrant

where would victories be, were it
    not for the defeat to be, forgiving and resilient
where would life be, were it
    not for the death to be, overly indulgent

ೞ♦ೞ

while there is still some humility left
recognize your own weaknesses
Once devoid, life will become
a dead-dried tree with many
holes and cracks

axes and saws are ever eager
to show-off their power

ೞ♦ೞ

Conflict -- Mukesh Chhajer

if you stumble, don't blame the path
    its innocence has caused it, many a heart breaks
if you get lost, don't blame the forest
    its generosity has become, a source of abuse
if you get cheated, don't blame the world
    do you have the courage, to look yourself in the mirror
if you meet failure, don't blame the means
    have you asked yourself, were the motives clean

ॐ♦ॐ

a thought can mutate in ways
it could never have imagined
by cannibalizing itself

bit-by-bit, selfishness
rises to the level of self righteousness
to drown out all possibilities
of a meaningful conversation

a shouting match between
deaf then ensues to fill the space
with, meaningless noise

explosions and gun shots don't
arise out of pure vacuum

ॐ♦ॐ

Conflict -- Mukesh Chhajer

death does not dream

what is there for it that it
is not able to achieve!!

ଔ♦ଞ

It is never an insult or a defeat
but the true understanding of the unwillingness
to acknowledge lack of one's own honesty
that destroys one's humanity

ଔ♦ଞ

thoughts, that do not even manage
to emerge from the dark cocoon
still rule lives
by mechanism, unknown

acts of utter absurdity, unparalleled cruelty
absolute compassion and unbelievable creativity
are just a few ways they surface
to let their presence be felt

ଔ♦ଞ

Conflict -- Mukesh Chhajer

to achieve half, you
              must be hasty
to reach full, take
              it easy

ॐ♦ॐ

big, sometimes is only as big
as the smallest heart it can
flow through

small, sometimes is only as small
as the largest smile it can
engender

truth, sometimes is only as true
as the smallest lie it can
expose

lie, sometimes is only as false
as the largest truth it can
suppress

ॐ♦ॐ

Conflict -- Mukesh Chhajer

warriors are those who do not surrender
against the strongest odds
unless, it is a child's smile

cowards are those who do not show mercy
under any circumstances
unless for their own benefit

wise are those who are
ever compassionate and forgiving
unless it is their own mistakes

fools are those who are
ever critical and disparaging
unless it is their own work

as the bulbs are getting brighter
darkness is finding it harder
to find places to retreat

one place though it knows
it can always count on is
a human heart

Conflict -- Mukesh Chhajer

I can call up a tomorrow
I can conjure a yesterday
my hands are tied though when
it comes to today

I can write a book
I can deliver a lecture
my hands are tied though when
it comes to silence

I can run a mile
I can exercise for an hour
my hands are tied though when
it comes to being still

ଓ♦ଵ

history has only one objective
to stay alive
A coat of truthfulness it wears
to make itself appear sacrosanct

easily deluding man in to
believing, its ancestry is pure
the soil though is saturated with
blood of countless innocent lives

ଓ♦ଵ

Conflict -- Mukesh Chhajer

how many tomorrows do you think
you can borrow before
you are declared, bankrupt

even nature has, its limitations

deep, where neither the land
nor the water or air can seep
lies the treasure that would
render all need for money
fame, power, and celebrity
meaningless

deep, where only way to reach
is through your breath
make it your friend and learn
to make it follow your lead

Conflict -- Mukesh Chhajer

I came tomorrow and departed yesterday
a reflection in the mirror though always
creates an image opposite

real is fake and false appears real
even birth and death have
switched their locations

is it any wonder then that man
engages in activities detrimental
to its own benefits

☙ ♦ ❧

don't embrace, what appears desirable
don't reject, what appears unpalatable
nature of the world is always duplicitous
first look within, to gain true meaning

☙ ♦ ❧

Conflict -- Mukesh Chhajer

as we recede into
the infinitesimal of the infinities
we become witnesses to
the vastness of life

like bursting universes emerging
out of cascading big bangs
without any desire to
take rest

except that man is too tightly wound around
its own circle of selfishness and greed
Taming infinities to put them back
into a cage, for mere display

☙ ♦ ❧

if you are not someone's yesterday
        you will soon be forgotten
if you are not someone's tomorrow
        in sorrow you will be alone
if you are not someone's support
        you are not worth much
world only measures one's value
        based upon what it can get, in return

☙ ♦ ❧

Conflict -- Mukesh Chhajer

sailing through isn't safe
walking through is even worse
no claim is routine in a life
full of hidden potholes

ಚ ♦ ಉ

every string is broken
                or loosely held
every bridge has become
                its own defense
every word is wavering
                to define its own meaning
when life stands
                at the verge of collapse
                            or renewal

ಚ ♦ ಉ

Conflict -- Mukesh Chhajer

today brought me no joy
            nor any sorrow
today only said, fill
            your own pot

unaccustomed though I am
            to separate myself from
yesterday and tomorrow
            tanks full of, muddy water

☙ ◆ ❧

as with truth and so with lies
too much sugar or too much salt
mind will suffer, body weakens
excess of either, demands price

☙ ◆ ❧

Conflict -- Mukesh Chhajer

wounds are not all alike

surface wounds even when deep
can heal with a scar to show for

wounds which fester within
can swallow a person without
seen even for a moment

ઝ ♦ ಬ

water runs only downhill
        unless you put a pump
a building will quickly crumble
        unless there is regular maintenance
a tree will become infected
        unless properly cared for
a truth will suffocate
        unless allowed fresh air

ઝ ♦ ಬ

Conflict -- Mukesh Chhajer

let there be no tomorrow
        with unfulfilled desires
let there be no yesterday
        with unsatiated sorrow
what you have today
        let it be the only claim
to spread it any further
        is to invite death

❦

hostile are neither thoughts
        nor actions
hostile is man, addicted
        to greed and selfishness

❦

Conflict -- Mukesh Chhajer

some resign, some get
                pushed out
some leave, some merely
                disappear
some remembered, some refuse
                to fade away
each goes its own separate way
                only after all transactions have been
                      settled

ఆ♦ఎ

About Author

Mukesh Chhajer teaches mathematics and physics in Danville VA. He holds a bachelor's and a master's degree in chemical engineering and a Ph.D. in polymer physics. He has previously published eighteen books: Twelve collections of poetry in English, Four collections of poems in Hindi, a biography of Mahavir Swami in verse and one book of essays on Jainism.

www.ingramcontent.com/pod-product-compliance
Lightning Source LLC
Chambersburg PA
CBHW060405050426
42449CB00009B/1913